BOMBING IRON

Osprey Colour Series

Michael O'Leary

BOMBING IRON

Airworthy bombers of WW2 and Korea

Published in 1987 by Osprey Publishing Limited
27A Floral Street, London WC2E 9DP
Member company of the George Philip Group

British Library Cataloguing in Publication Data

Bombing iron; airworthy bombers of WW2 and Korea.—
   (Osprey Colour Series)
   1. Bombers—History—Pictorial works
   I. O'Leary, Michael
   623.74'63'09044   UG1242.B6

ISBN 0-85045-765-3

Editor Dennis Baldry
Designed by Paul Butters
Printed in Hong Kong

Front cover B-17G *Sentimental Journey* settles in
for landing at Madera, California. There are many
airshows in America, Britain and Europe where
vintage bombers are flown. Most speciality
aviation publications list these events well in
advance

Back cover Currently in the final stages of a
painstaking restoration by the Canadian Warplane
Heritage, this Lancaster Mk X, serial FM213,
should be joining the airshow circuit in the
summer of 1988

Title pages Down and dirty. With flaps and gear
down, Jack Spanich pilots his Douglas AD-4NA
Skyraider towards a landing at Space Center
Executive Airport, Titusville, Florida, during the
1983 edition of the Valiant Air Command's annual
warbird airshow. Spanich was one of the first
owner/pilots to restore a warbird in Vietnam-era
camouflage and markings

Right A dubious Bruce Guberman looks on as
the author pilots *Executive Sweet* through
Southern California smog while on the way to a
photo assignment. Guberman, an FAA examiner
in the B-25 and A-26, as well as being type rated
in the B-17, was the photo plane pilot for the
majority of photographs in *Bombing Iron*. To get
the needed aerial photographs a wide variety of
aircraft types were employed as camera ships,
including the Mitchell, Beech Bonanza, C-45 and
AT-11 Kansan; Piper Saratoga and Seneca; North
American AT-6 Texan and P-51D Mustang.
(Photograph by Rick Richmond)

It's really by chance that the few WW2 bombers still flying today survived the mass aircraft scrappings following the conclusion of the war, a time when America was trying to convert its swords into ploughshares. Perhaps it is only in America that these aircraft could have survived. Some companies had a need for four engine bombers (photo mapping platforms, cargo haulers, or gun runners) while the medium bombers found new careers in aerial application, fire bombing, and, later, conversion into high speed executive transports.

The task of restoring a vintage bombing aircraft and bringing it back to WW2 configuration is daunting at best. The availability of original parts such as turrets has become difficult (not to mention expensive) while other problems such as liability insurance and the decreasing availability of avgas are major issues facing the warbird community.

Currently, many fine examples of restored WW2 and Korean War aircraft grace our skies. This book attempts to illustrate a few of them and recall an era in history whose lessons, hopefully, will not be forgotten.

Michael O'Leary
Los Angeles June 1987

Michael O'Leary is employed as Editor and Associate Publisher for a group of aviation-related magazines. Operating from Los Angeles, the author has had the opportunity to fly in many different types of aircraft. His favourite aircraft are the classic machines from the Second World War—the ultimate piston-engine warplanes.

Bomber restorer's paradise! This September 1980 view shows just a portion of David Tallichet's vast warbird holdings at Chino, California. Tallichet, a collector who has travelled the world in search of rare and exotic WW2 aircraft, has restored a number of planes to flying condition but, unfortunately, none of the aircraft in this view. The disassembled Douglas A-20 Havoc in the foreground was recovered from Nicaragua shortly before the current *Sandinista* regime clamped down on most activities (including, one would surmise, the collecting of old warbirds!). Records do not show any evidence of Havocs operating with the *Fuerza Aerea de Nicaragua* and it would be interesting if the vintage attack bomber could talk. Other aircraft in the background include a vandalized Mitchell from *Catch-22*, a Bristol Bolingbroke, an ultra-rare Curtiss SB2C Helldiver, and a TBM-3 Avenger

Contents

Medium cool

Mitch the Witch head-on over the mountains north of Chino, California. Photographed from the back of another Mitchell with the gunner's armour glass removed, Bob Pond's freshly restored B-25J had been redone by Steve Hinton's Fighter Rebuilders. The aircraft is painted in the colourful markings of an actual Mitchell of the 17th Tactical Reconnaissance Bomb Squadron that, on 25 February 1944, took on a Japanese *Sally* medium bomber in a bomber version of a dogfight near Kavieng, New Ireland. The Mitchell won

Overleaf, inset The gaily painted vertical tail of *Mitch the Witch*. The insignia of the 17th Tactical Recon Bomb Squadron (known as the 'Fighting 17th') is clearly illustrated. Bob Pond's Mitchell divides its time between his museum in Minnesota and Southern California where it can often be seen at Chino and Palm Springs

Overleaf 'Mitchell, break right now!' *Mitch the Witch* thunders away from the camera plane at the conclusion of the May 1986 photo flight. This view shows a number of details to advantage including the bomb bay doors, dual landing lights, and the tail 'bumper' at the rear of the fuselage

9

Painted in the US Navy's version of Olive Drab, N333RW rumbles down the taxiway at Breckenridge, Texas, during the field's annual May airshow during 1986. Painted as a USN PBJ-1J, the ultra-clean Mitchell well-represents the USN and US Marine Corps' heavy usage of the Mitchell during WW2 in the South Pacific. This Mitchell is owned and operated by The Lone Star Aviation Museum, Houston, Texas

Inset From being either workhorses or unwanted eyesores not that many years ago, today's *Bombing Iron* aircraft are revered veterans of history's most tumultuous conflict. Accordingly, owners are going to great lengths to make sure their charges are maintained in pristine condition—both mechanically and aesthetically. Paint jobs for the big bombers cost many thousands of dollars and are certainly of much better quality than when the aircraft were made! This detail view shows some of the work that went into N333RW, including a very nice Varga girl applied ahead of the two .50 calibre Browning 'package' guns. Alberto Vargas (note the 's' which was quite often dropped from his art work) painted attractive women for the pages of *Esquire* and other publications that became the inspiration for a generation of fighting men. The fact that copies of his seductive females adorned countless combat aircraft was 'one of my proudest achievements', said Vargas in an interview with the author shortly before the artist's death

Pilot John H Bell II brings Mitchell *Heavenly Body* N8195H (TB-25N, s/n 44-30748, c/n 108-35073) in for a close look at the camera plane. Owned by Mike Pupich and based at Van Nuys, California, this Mitchell is an ex-*Catch-22* film star and has been the subject of much loving care lavished by a band of volunteers over the past few years. The large metal patch on the top fuselage behind the cockpit is a covering over where the top gun turret was installed. During the 1950s, most surviving military Mitchells had the turret and its mounting ring removed since the bomber no longer had a combat role and was used mainly for transport and training duties. Unfortunately, the mounting ring and turret are now extremely difficult (and expensive) to find. The Eagle Field decal denotes the fact that Pupich and other warbird lovers are trying to develop a WW2 civilian pilot training (CPT) airport known as Eagle Field, located in California's central valley, into an all-warbird base

Overleaf Glowing with the golden light of a setting California sun, Bruce Guberman holds *Executive Sweet* in formation with Ascher Ward's Texan camera plane. N30801 (ex-N3699G) is a B-25J, AAF s/n 44-30801, c/n 108-34076, that led a varied life after being surplused from USAF service. After a bout of spraying bugs, the Mitchell became the lead B-25 for the epic film *Catch-22*. When the film was completed the Mitchells were sold off for bargain-basement prices (remember, this was in the early 1970s when few individuals had much use for a fuel-hungry twin-engine bomber). Purchased by publisher and veteran pilot Ed Schnepf, the bomber was brought back to pristine warbird condition as the first of a whole new generation of restored and rebuilt ex-WW2 bombing aircraft. The Mitchell is now under the ownership of the American Aeronautical Foundation Museum. Note the open bomb bay doors

Left B-25J N5865V, its big Wright R-2600 radials nicely synchronized, cruises over the Houston countryside. Most Mitchell restorers favour the glass nose since an extra passenger can be carried. The B-25J was the final production variant of the Mitchell and 4318 were built (not counting 72 further examples scrapped on the production line at the end of the war). The B-25J could carry 3200 lbs of bombs and 13 .50 calibre air-cooled Browning machine guns

Below *Big Ole Brew 'n Little Ole You* is an appropriate name for this restored Mitchell. The B-25's controls are operated purely by 'muscle' power and it can be a tiring aircraft to fly—especially in formation or in poor weather. Beautifully framed by a Texas thunderhead at the September 1986 Wings Over Houston airshow, N5865V is a B-25J, s/n 44-30988, c/n 108-34263, which was restored by Mitchell rebuilder Tom Reilly who specializes in bringing basketcase B-25s back to life. Today's detailed restorations are seeing the addition of such items as operable upper gun turrets

The Canadian Warplane Heritage, based at Mt Hope, Hamilton, Ontario, maintain one of the finest collections of flying WW2 aircraft. One of the stars of their fleet is this B-25J, C-GCWM, which had been previously used by Bendix as an executive aircraft and test bed. Since being acquired by the CWH in the mid-1970s, the Mitchell has been a flying restoration—gradually being restored to WW2 configuration while being kept operational. When our October 1976 photo was taken the CWH still had not added the upper gun turret or the full compliment of nose weapons. Today, the beautifully finished bomber reflects the pride and care that the CWH lavishes on its fleet of vintage warriors

Overleaf As previously mentioned, the movie version of Joseph Heller's (who was a WW2 Mitchell crewman) famous novel *Catch-22* was responsible for saving the majority of America's Mitchells—most of which, by the time the movie began to be made in 1968, had lapsed either into dereliction or, at best, semi-flyable condition. Eighteen Mitchells were made flyable, fitted with fake turrets and given fanciful military camouflage schemes. The bombers were then flown *en masse* to the filming location in Mexico. After their return to the Tallmantz facility at Orange County, California, where the rebuilding work had taken place, the bombers were sold off by the studio at prices ranging from a mere $3000 to $6000! B-25J *Denver Dumper* is seen waiting for a buyer at Orange County on 29 June 1969—note the piles of Mitchell parts and spares surrounding the B-25

Top left With its left engine 'caged', *In the Mood* heads back to its home field at Chino, California. N9117Z is a B-25J, s/n 44-29199, s/n 108-32474, that is basically a 'plain jane'—without turret, guns, or much in the way of decoration except for some nice nose art

Left Painted in attractive post-WW2 Royal Canadian Air Force No 418 'City of Edmonton' Squadron, this B-25J, 45-8884, was photographed over Madera, California, during August 1982. Owned by Jerry Janes and registered in Canada as C-GCWJ, the aircraft had previously been N3156G. The RCAF acquired seventy-five B-25Js from surplus USAF stocks in 1951 in order to supplement seventy Mitchell IIIs that had previously been obtained from the RAF. These B-25Js saw service until 1963, about the time the USAF was retiring its last Mitchells which had been used as personnel transports and trainers

Above One of the finest Mitchells flying belonged to Dr John Marshall. N10564 (B-25J, s/n 44-29887, c/n 108-33162) is an ex-*Catch-22* veteran and former Forest Service fire bomber and was not in the best shape when acquired by Dr Marshall. Thousands of manhours and lots of money helped create one of the finest replicas of a combat-operational WW2 bomber with original internal equipment including original radios, bombs, guns, bombsights, etc. Painted in desert camouflage and markings, the Mitchell was a regular visitor to many East Coast airshows. Unfortunately no longer flying, the Mitchell was donated to the National Air and Space Museum and is currently in storage at Dulles Airport, waiting the construction of a new NASM building where it will be displayed along with many other NASM treasures which are also kept in storage

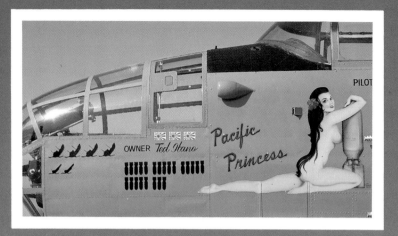

It's not as easy as it looks! Formation flying in the Mitchell is a very demanding task, requiring constant attention to the heavy controls and throttles for the Wright R-2600s. On a hot and bumpy day over California's central valley, Carl Scholl leads a pack of Mitchells in very tight formation. Painted as a US Navy -BJ-1J, the lead TB-25N (N9856C, 43-28204) is owned by Ted Itano and based at Chino, California

Inset Close-up of the well-done nose art on Ted Itano's *Pacific Princess*. This view also shows the swivel mounted .50 calibre Browning machine gun and Norden bombsight. TB-25Ns were Mitchells overhauled in the 1950s by Hayes Aircraft for the USAF to use as trainers

Above In tight formation. Tom Crevasse pilots Harry Doan's camouflaged Mitchell in close formation with the Beech AT-11 camera plane. This aircraft had been an abandoned cargo freighter but was restored to flying condition by Doan and his crew in Florida. The Mitchell is a B-25J, registered N9621C (s/n 45-8811). With today's current values, a fully restored B-25 brings around $250,000 on the warbird market.

Top right Pushing the throttles for the R-2600s a bit forward, Tom Crevasse breaks away from the camera plane and heads back to the Space Center Executive Airport during the May 1987 Valiant Air Command show. A few weeks later, Tom skillfully crash landed another Mitchell in the Everglades swamp near the airfield. Both engines on the Mitchell failed but, by using his considerable piloting skills, Tom got the bomber down with a minimum amount of damage to the airframe and no injuries to the passengers

Right Beautifully polished Mitchell *Georgia Mae* NL5262V is owned and flown by Wiley Sanders of Troy, Alambama. Wiley must like Mitchells, he owns two of them—this glass-nose example and a solid nose 'strafer' variant. Most pilots who fly the Mitchell describe the aircraft as being like a giant Piper Cub—except when an engine quits!

Turretless B-25J N9643C (s/n 44-86758, c/n 108-47512) is flown by the Confederate Air Force and done up as a United States Marine Corps PBJ-1J Mitchell operated by VMB-612. Surplus Mitchells have been used for a wide variety of tasks—as fire bombers, fish freighters and drug runners. Fortunately, on any given day, around two dozen to thirty Mitchells are still capable of taking to the air and this number is slowly growing thanks to such outfits like Aero Trader at Chino Airport who not only restore Mitchells back to flying shape but maintain a huge parts inventory (gathered from sources all around the world) that helps keep the operational B-25s flying

Right One of the hardest-working attack bombers of WW2 was the Douglas A-20 Havoc series, fighting with American forces all the way through the conflict. However, only two examples of the aircraft remain flyable (out of 7098 examples built by Douglas and 380 by Boeing) while only a handful are on display in museums around the world. Found as a derelict airframe, William Farrah of El Paso, Texas, put several years of intensive labour into getting this A-20G back into flying condition. The A-20G variant of the attack bomber is powered by two Wright R-2600 radials and is capable of a top speed of 315 mph

During WW2, the USAAF's famous 'Air Apaches' caused constant havoc among Japanese shipping and airfields in the Pacific. Skimming in at tree-top or wave top height, the Mitchells of the Air Apaches hit the enemy with withering concentrations of .50 calibre machine gun fire and loads or fragmentation bombs. This Mitchell, owned by Tom Thompson, is restored in dramatic Air Apache colours. Note the operational top turret tracking the camera plane!

One of the most neglected of all warbird bombers is the Lockheed PV-2 Ventura, 500 of which were built at Burbank, California, starting in mid-1943. The Harpoon was a heavy-hitter, built for the US Navy's attack bomber role. Carrying up to ten .50 calibre machine guns, eight 5-inch rockets and a heavy bomb load, Harpoons attacked and destroyed Japanese targets all across the warfront—quite often engaging and defeating the vaunted Mitsubishi Zero. Used by the Naval Reserves after the war, most Harpoons quietly disappeared to the scrappers but many were

converted to high-speed executive transports while others were employed as fire bombers and bug sprayers. Only catching on as a collectable warbird in the early 1980s, around a half dozen Harpoons are currently under restoration to full military configuration. This example (N7255C, Buno 37257) was quietly rotting away with several other Harpoons at Douglas, Arizona, in 1970— unfortunately indicative, at the time, of the interest in a warplane that had seen considerable action in the defence of its country

Left *Fat Cat* is a restored Lockheed PV-2 Harpoon with an interesting history. N7428C, after being surplused from US Navy service, went through several different owners before being sent to Dee Howard Aircraft in Texas for extensive modification. The new owners wanted the Harpoon heavily modified for use as a freighter to bring rare plants from Latin America to the States. Accordingly contracted to Dee Howard in 1965, a leading aircraft modifier, the Harpoon's interior was gutted and a large cargo door was cut into the right side of the fuselage. The most interesting aspect of the modification was the fact that the fuselage was stretched by four feet

Inset N7428C's career as a freighter was short-lived. The modification was extremely expensive, around $200,000, and the market for rare plants apparently not as extensive as the new owners thought. After passing through more owners, the Harpoon began a new career as a drug runner. Eventually impounded, the PV-2 was purchased by Richard Mitchell of New Iberia, Louisiana. A group of volunteers active in the Cajun Wing of the Confederate Air Force began getting their big bird ready to fly again and this was no small task since the Harpoon had been more than mistreated. The airplane was eventually put into ferry condition and has been the subject of a working

restoration. As can be seen in our photos, *Fat Cat* has been nicely polished and some military details like machine gun barrels and underwing rockets have been added. Flown by Richard Mitchell and Bob DeRosier, the bomber is now an airshow regular

Above Chino Airport in Southern California is the home of many exotic warbirds. David Tallichet's Yesterday's Air Force holds upwards of 150 aircraft and airframes awaiting restoration. Perhaps one of the rarest aircraft in Tallichet's monumental collection is this Martin B-26 Marauder. One of three recovered by Tallichet from the wilds of Canada in the early 1970s, the Marauders had gone down after becoming lost on a ferry flight and running low on fuel. One was badly damaged in the accident but the other two remained relatively undamaged, the cold Canadian climate keeping the metal and paint work in a remarkable state of preservation. One example was selected for restoration after having been transferred back to Chino and the short-wing Marauder is seen as restoration began in 1977. Today, the aircraft is physically complete and only detail work remains to be finished before the rare bomber is ready to fly once again

Top right Unless a surplus bomber had a very specific use or very caring owner, most surviving examples were rapidly heading on their way downhill during the early 1960s when there was little use for the fuel hungry veterans. The first executive jets were just coming on the market so many of the transport conversions were being dumped in favour of the more practical (and more glamorous) new Learjets. This Douglas A-26B Invader is seen in a sad state at Fresno, California. Basically in stock condition, the Invader still retains its overall black night intruder camouflage, the white being added by the civilian owners. N9432Z is not carried on current civil registers so the old warhorse was probably scrapped sometime after being photographed during May 1968

This Martin Marauder has been a hard-luck warbird but it has managed to survive a number of misfortunes. Surplused immediately after the conclusion of the war, N5546N was turned into a cross-country racer and flown as the *Valley Turtle*. Not particularly successful, the B-26 was then sold for conversion to executive status and the modifications were extensive including a new nose and tail section, deluxe interior, airstair door, and new props and cowlings. Used by an oil company, the plane was later sold in Mexico as XB-LOX. Returned to the States in the late 1960s, the plane was damaged in a landing accident and acquired by the CAF. After being moved to Harlingen, the Marauder was very heavily damaged when the gear retracted while rolling (note the bent wing and other damage). After being stored, the CAF decided to raise funds to try to restore the Marauder back to wartime configuration. It took years but the prooect was finally completed—only to have the nose gear collapse on touchdown during a 1986 show. The Marauder has again been repaired and is, currently, the only flying example of Martin's famous fast bomber

Right Considered to be the ultimate Invader, a row of On-Mark B-26K Counter Invaders is seen awaiting scrapping at Davis-Monthan AFB during September 1971. Stock Invaders held in storage by the USAF were completely redone at Van Nuys, California, by On-Mark during the early 1960s for operations in Southeast Asia. New, powerful R-2800 CB-17 engines were installed along with new spars, strengthened wings and new avionics. The planes were given new serials (this example being 64-17671) and then flown to Southeast Asia where they were employed on a variety of heavy-duty missions against the communists—many of the missions being clandestine. After their military use, the government did not want the planes to be sold surplus to civilians and most of the battle-hardened veterans were cut up for scrap metal. However, a couple did survive and one Counter Invader has been restored to operational condition in Montana. This particular machine went to the Forest Service where it did not become operational and was then passed to the Florence Air Museum, South Carolina

Above Updated to B-26K configuration, *Forca Aerea Brasileira* B-26C (note that the old designation was retained) 5174 awaits an engine run at Hamilton. Camouflaged glossy green and grey, the Invader has two under wing weapon pylons as well as rocket rails. Wings are fitted for six .50 calibre Browning machine guns. Photographed in May 1969, the rebuilt Invaders went on to serve Brazil for ten years before being retired

Below In the late 1960s, Brazil decided to have its fleet of Invaders upgraded to basic B-26K configuration. By this time On-Mark had gone on to other projects so a license for the conversion work was issued to Hamilton Aircraft in Tucson, Arizona. The Brazilian Invaders were ferried north and modifications were undertaken on a production line basis. Stripped of its engines, B-26C 5159 is seen awaiting conversion. Note underwing gun pods and rocket rails

Polished like a mirror, VB-26C 0-34610 is seen on the ramp at Edwards AFB during May 1972. Operated by the National Guard Bureau out of Washington, DC, this Invader (along with a couple of others) was employed as a VIP transport for ranking Air National Guard officers. Declining availability of parts and increasing difficulty in obtaining avgas forced the retirement of these classics by the mid-1970s

Top right Two classics bask in the Arizona sun! Invader B-26C N9996Z receives some work to the tail cone area while the mechanic's '55 Cadillac stands guard. Photographed at Deer Valley Airport on 5 April 1968, the Invader was being operated as a fire bomber with the Forest Service area code 11C painted on the vertical tail. The Invader has enjoyed a long life as a fire bomber, the power from the Pratt & Whitney R-2800s being particularly appreciated by pilots operating with heavy chemical loads in very hot environments

Right Ready to race. During the late 1950s and 1960s, On-Mark Engineering at Van Nuys, California, established itself as the leading modifier of Douglas Invaders into executive transports. On-Mark completely redid the basic airframe, adding new ring spars which permitted higher operational speeds as well as allowing passengers to stand more or less upright in the cabin. CB-17 engines added super high horsepower while the deluxe versions had cabin pressurization, providing the ultimate in pre-Learjet executive transportation. Once the jets came into operation, the On-Marks were quickly dumped onto the open market, usually at very low prices. A young Pan American pilot by the name of Lloyd Hamilton purchased On-Mark N500M and raced the beast at the 1971 Mojave, California, air races where the powerful twin did fairly well for itself. Race 16 is seen ready for the next round at Mojave with its extra long executive nose and tip tanks. The aircraft currently exists in different ownership and in poor condition

Well-armed guards puzzle on why some crazy gringos want to fly this marginally airworthy Invader out of Tegucigalpa, Honduras, during December 1982. This aircraft was the only Invader used by the *Fuerza Aerea Hondurena* and was eventually put up for sale following the acquisition of more modern equipment. This Invader, s/n 44-35918 c/n 29197, was obtained from Costa Rica in 1969 where it had been carried on the civil register as TI-1040P. Given the Honduran civil register of HR-276, the attack bomber was transferred to the FAH as 276 in 1971. This serial later became FAH-510

Inset After sitting idle for several years, the R-2800s on FAH-510 burst into life on the first try. After several test flights at Tegucigalpa, Mike and Dick Wright and Dave Zeuschel flew the Invader to Texas where it was put on permanent static display at a USAF base. The vintage bomber performed quite well on its ferry flight which was good since some of the territory flown over was inhabited by rather primitive natives who had the occasional hankering for a nice chunk of human

During the 1970s, Invaders could be purchased for small amounts of money. Their high top speed and long range made them ideal candidates for drug runners. Numerous aircraft were either wrecked, impounded or abandoned while engaged in this activity. The Waco Wing of the Confederate Air Force obtained their Invader after it had been used for various nefarious activities. Lots of money and volunteer labour were poured into N250P to bring it back to flying condition and the rather impressive result can be seen in this photo as N240P sits on the ramp at Breckenridge, Texas, during May 1983

Overleaf Gun-nose A-26B Invaders await their airshow flights at the annual Breckenridge, Texas, warbird gathering. N240P, in the foreground, is finished in the overall black night intruder markings while N26RP, in the background, is finished in glossy olive drab. Both aircraft had been converted into executive transports during the late 1950s or early 1960s as can be seen by the airstair entrance doors located in the area formerly occupied by the bomb bay

Discovered in the early 1980s in a derelict
condition in Brazil, this Invader was
purchased by the Tired Iron Racing Team in
Casper, Wyoming. After purchase, only one
problem remained . . . getting the plane back
to the United States! Mike and Dick Wright
travelled to Brazil where they spent months
bringing the old bird back to life

The Wright brothers got the Brazilian
Invader into flyable shape with the addition
of two new R-2800s and lots of labour. This
aircraft had served with the *Forca Aerea
Brasileira* and was one of the Invaders
modified by Hamilton Aircraft in Arizona.
After passing from active service, the
airframe was basically abandoned.
Fortunately, the ferry flight back to the
States went smoothly and the Invader's
restoration was completely finished. The
resulting fine product, named *Puss & Boots*, is
seen turning final at Breckenridge. Gear
speed on the Invader is 160 mph and final
approach is flown at 130 mph with full down
flaps

Insets, left to right 1 Low over the Texas
scrub, *Puss & Boots* settles in for its final
approach, nose held high and flaps full down.
2 Lined up on the centreline at Breckenridge,
Puss & Boots approaches the threshold. 3
Throttles come back to 15 inches manifold
pressure and speed to 105 mph as *Puss &
Boots* prepares to join its shadow on the
runway

The sleek, deadly lines of the Invader are seen over California farmland during August 1985. The twin turrets on the Invader were remotely controlled by a gunner sitting under a glass enclosure to the rear of the fuselage. The gunner operated the electrically-driven turrets by a pair of handgrips attached to a periscope sight (the top of which can be seen projecting from the gunner's position). The A-26C packed up to 16 .50 calibre machine guns during WW2 and Korea. The restored *Whistler's Mother* made its first flight after total restoration on 15 August 1983 with Bruce Guberman at the controls. This flight did not go smoothly—the landing gear failed to lower! After circling Fox Field, Lancaster, California, for a few hours, mechanic Nelson Knuedeler managed to find the source of trouble and corrected the hydraulic problem—allowing the gear to lower

Left B-26C 41-39401 was purchased by film maker Dick Moore when the Invader was surplused in 1958. The plane was flown to Van Nuys Airport in California where it became a local, decidedly non-flying, landmark. During the 1960s, the Invader was put back into the air briefly for its movie role. The interesting point about this aircraft was the fact that it had never been demilitarized. All the original military equipment, including the turrets, was still fully operational. During the late 1970s, the bomber attracted the attention of Ed Schnepf and the American Aeronautical Foundation Museum. The aircraft was transferred to the AAF and an intensive restoration project was undertaken, a task comprising five years and 5000 man-hours. Head of the detailed restoration was Nelson Knuedeler who did an outstanding job insuring that every function of the bomber was brought back to military standard

Upper inset The heart of the Invader's incredible reserve of power: two mighty Pratt & Whitney R-2800 radials capable of giving a top speed of 355 mph at 15,000 ft. Very reliable engines, the P&Ws were one of the main reasons that the Invader came out of the European air war losing only 67 of its type in combat. N39401 flew thirty combat missions in Europe before being returned to the States following VE Day. Its peacetime rest was to be brief, however, and the Invader (redesignated B-26 in 1947) went to war in Korea—flying a further 100 combat missions. Returned once again to the States, the B-26C was eventually transferred to the 180th Tactical Reconnaissance Squadron of the Missouri Air National Guard and based at St Joseph

Lower inset The Douglas Invader combined fighter-like performance with excellent visibility as seen in this photograph of Bruce Guberman taking *Whistler's Mother* down low over the Pacific at 275 mph. Although quite a large aircraft, the cockpit of the Invader is cramped, especially the jump seat from which this photograph was taken

Above The fanciful artwork on the side of *Whistler's Mother* is not a recreation of a WW2 artist's handiwork but, rather, the insignia applied for a movie of the same name when the aircraft was restored to flight for the first time in the 1960s under the ownership of film maker Dick Moore for his WW2 epic. S/n 41-39401 was one of 1086 such models built at the Douglas factory in Tulsa, Oklahoma. This particular Invader had seen combat over Europe with the 643rd Bomb Squadron, 409th Bomb Group, where its heavy machine gun punch and carriage of up to 4000 lbs of weapons quickly proved their worth

With its massive tricycle gear lowered, *Whistler's Mother* practices slow flight shortly after restoration. At this point (August 1983) the four underwing gun packs (each housing two .50 calibre machine guns) had not been installed. Most Invaders were delivered with just one set of controls but the AAF Museum wanted N39401 to have dual controls. Nelson Knuedeler visited Davis-Monthan AFB when the Counter-Invader fleet was being scrapped and obtained a dual control cockpit section, the controls of which were incorporated into 41-39401

Inset This view shows the bottom turret on the A-26C to advantage. With its high top speed (airframe was redlined at 425 mph but this was quite often exceeded in the heat of combat) and heavy armament, the Invader often met and defeated enemy fighters

Top right With the massive bomb doors open, the Invader makes for an impressive sight. The doors could be opened right up to red line speed. Note the barely visible spoilers in front of the doors that automatically lower as the doors open. The spoilers break up the airflow in front of the doors, making sure that the bombs can fall freely from the bay. On later variants of the A-26C (from the C-45-DT block on), the Invader had three .50 calibres mounted internally in each outer wing panel

Right N39401 gracefully breaks away from the camera aircraft. Aside from being involved in three major wars (WW2, Korea, Vietnam), Invaders have seen action in many of the world's hot spots including mercenary action in Africa, numerous Latin American 'problems', and in the infamous Bay of Pigs invasion. Today, a stock Invader is an extremely rare warbird since the majority of surviving airframes tend to be various 'flavours' of the many different executive modifications done in the 1950s and early 1960s. Most probably, *Whistler's Mother* will remain as the prime example of an operationally restored Invader. In late 1985, ownership of the Invader passed to Kermit Weeks and the aircraft is now on display in his newly opened Weeks Air Museum, Tamiami Airport, Miami, Florida, where it is kept in flying condition

Bomber moderne

In order to create a high speed medium bomber for the United States Army Air Corps, Douglas Aircraft Corporation, Santa Monica, California, created a rather elegant new design that utilized the wings of the DC-3 commercial transport. Ordered in late 1938, the new B-23 was first flown on 27 July 1939. Although the new aircraft had a top speed of 282 mph, the design had many shortcomings when compared to the four-engined Boeing B-17 as well as being slower than the new B-25 and B-26. Only thirty-eight B-23s were built. However, the limited production design did introduce a manned tail gunner's position with a single .50 calibre machine gun—the first such installation on a 'modern' American bomber

Overleaf The B-23 Dragon was a rather pleasing aircraft with its swept-back wings and larger vertical tail. However, the aircraft saw little operational use and around two dozen were quickly converted to UC-67 transports. After the war, surviving B-23s were snapped up for conversion to plush executive transports. One of the largest purchaser of surplus Dragons was Howard Hughes, who held a fascination for the Douglas product. In the executive role, the Dragon could carry up to twelve passengers in two compartments. This example, N4000B, is owned by the Weeks Air Museum, Miami, Florida, and will be the subject of a future in-depth restoration

Overleaf, inset Close-up view of N4000B shows the rather tatty condition of this particular Dragon. Converted after the war into an executive transport, N4000B will eventually be fully converted back to its wartime configuration by the ambitious Weeks Air Museum. Many Dragons had a larger, more streamlined, nose installed during conversion but N4000B, fortunately, still retains its original short nose complete with framing for the bombardier. As a historical footnote, Jimmy Doolittle picked the B-23 as his first choice for the strike on Tokyo. However, the Dragon's wingspan would not clear the *Hornet's* island

Right One of the more utilized Dragons is N747M (s/n 39-33, c/n 2719), seen here at Monterrey, California, during May 1974 when the transport was finished in a rather fanciful—but appropriate—paint scheme. This Dragon, once the personal mount of Howard Hughes, later passed into the ownership of the colourful and eccentric Ed Daley, owner of World Airways. Daley had the aircraft completely refurbished, the paint stripped and the aluminium skin polished until it glowed. Daley added some pre-war Air Corps markings along with the painting of a leprauchan to denote his heritage. Following Daley's death, the ex-bomber has been placed on long-term loan to the Douglas Aircraft Museum and the plane is currently housed at the Douglas facility at Long Beach, California

Left During the 1960s and 1970s, the surviving Dragons fell upon hard times as the need for surplus converted WW2 bombers quickly dried up. Several B-23s were destroyed in drug runs while others lapsed into dereliction. N33311 was donated to Los Angeles Trade Tech—an aviation vocational school—where it was used by the students as a teaching aid. Student protests and the general violence that marred the late 1960s took a toll on N33311 when the plane was set afire by a vandal. The results are apparent as the ruined Dragon is seen during May 1969. The B-25 (nose just visible) also used by the school was scrapped not long afterwards

In a rather curious footnote to history, one Douglas Dragon went to work for the military again—some thirty years after being declared surplus. N52327 (s/n 39-36, c/n 2722) was operated by the University of Washington for the Air Force Cambridge Research Laboratory. With a crew of five engineers and two pilots, the aircraft was used to simple cloud particles under a project headed by the Advanced Ballistic Reentry Systems Program Office. Unfortunately, in 1984, N52327 was heavily damaged in a landing accident at Kingman, Arizona (the site of the mass scrapping of the majority of America's WW2 bombing fleet). It appeared that the rare Dragon was going to head for the scrap heap but the plane was rescued by aeronautical horse trader Ascher Ward who had big plans for the damaged Dragon

Inset Ward and his crew of workers got N52327 patched up at Kingman and flew the aircraft to Mojave where more extensive repairs were undertaken, including the building of a 'bomber' nose to replace the more streamlined executive modification. The Dragon was ferried to McChord AFB as part of a trade with the USAF Museum. McChord had actually operated Dragons and the rebuilt aircraft has become part of the base's heritage museum. The Dragon, sprayed in Air Corps markings, was ferried to McChord with its gear locked down

One of the least attractive of the Air Corps new generation of 'modern' bombers was the portly Douglas B-18 Bolo. In May 1934, the Air Corps announced a competition for a new bomber that was to carry 2000 lbs of bombs for 1000 miles (preferably 2000 miles) at a top speed of at least 200 mph (preferably 250 mph). Douglas decided to build a bombing aircraft around the wings of a DC-2 transport. The fat-bellied bomber was first flown in August 1935 as the DB-1 and the plane was put into competition with other contemporary bombers including the Boeing 299 (to become the B-17). The Army, mistakenly, reasoned that since the DB-1 cost $58,500 compared to the Boeing's $99,620,

then it would be better to order more Douglas aircraft. An order was drafted for 133 B-18s and thirteen YB-17s. The B-18 was a ponderous looking machine and, besides having examples shot to pieces in Hawaii and the Philippines during the initial Japanese attacks, the type did not see combat except for coastal patrols looking for submarines. Surplus B-18s were purchased for use as cargo aircraft and crop sprayers. N56867, a B-18A, is seen languishing among a collection of doomed Constellations during May 1969 at Tucson, Arizona. This aircraft had been fitted as a sprayer and, fortunately, survives today as part of the USAF Museum collection

Douglas B-18B N66267, s/n 39-2643, retains the bulbous nose that once housed a radar unit for coastal sub patrol. This particular Bolo, as the type was named, led a long and hazardous life as a fire bomber and crop sprayer before eventually being obtained by the USAF Museum for display

Heavyweight champions

Left Queen of the skies. If there is one single aircraft that captures public imagination when bombing aircraft of WW2 are discussed, then that aircraft is the Boeing B-17 Flying Fortress. Our leading photograph depicts *Sentimental Journey*, A B-17G (s/n 44-83514, c/n 32155, N9323Z) owned and operated by the Arizona Wing of the Confederate Air Force. *Sentimental Journey* is probably the most authentically restored Fortress still flying

During 1986, Aviation Specialities, a large fire bombing and aerial applicator company, decided to auction off its collection of vintage workhorses. Included in this collection were four operational B-17 Flying Fortresses. Fortunately, all these aircraft were purchased by caring collectors who are now bringing the machines back to stock WW2 condition. One of the most ambitious groups is the National Warplane Museum in Geneseo, New York, who obtained N9563Z (s/n 44-83563, c/n 32204) and flew it back to their home airfield where the aircraft is being kept in operational condition while restoration work continues

Its fading and chipped civilian paint work stripped off and its aluminium skin polished, N9563Z made one of its first airshow outings at the June 1986 Canadian Warplane Heritage event. By this time, an early model top turret had been installed and much mechanical work had been carried out. During its career, a cargo door had been installed in the right side of the fuselage and this will eventually be removed. N9563Z is a veteran of the 1961 film *The War Lover* as well as the later *Tora! Tora! Tora!*

Inset N9563Z cruises over the Canadian countryside. As can be seen, the nose glass was in extremely poor condition when purchased and this will eventually be replaced. The National Warplane Museum hopes to obtain a complete selection of gun turrets and will eventually paint their big bird in an accurate WW2 paint scheme

Above Unusual view of a Flying Fortress in formation. In October 1977, Aero Union, a Chico, California, based fire bomber outfit, brought one of their Forts, N9323Z, to the Confederate Air Force annual show at Harlingen, Texas. In hopes of selling the veteran bomber, Aero Union applied some stars and bars along with the name *Class of '44* (the large red areas are visibility aids during retardant drops). Asking price was in the vicinity of $55,000 for the fire bomber which was in anything but stock condition. However, Aero Union's Forts were always maintained in superior condition and the price was more than a bargain. N9323Z was sold and, of course, eventually became the fabulous *Sentimental Journey*. This view is of interest because it shows the Fort with every nook and cranny filled with passengers. Note how the top hatch from the radio compartment has been removed and how the passengers are standing up in relative comfort, the hump of the top fuselage apparently blocking the airflow

Top right Forts have returned to the United States from some exotic foreign locales. This B-17G last saw service with the Brazilian Air Force where it was used for search and rescue (SAR) missions. Maintained over the years in good condition, the Fort was finally retired and sat for several years before being obtained by David Tallichet's Yesterday's Air Force. Photographed at Chino, California, during October 1977, s/n 44-83663 (FAB 5400) where, with crew door open, the aircraft sits ready for a flight

Right The fine condition of *Sentimental Journey* is reflected in this view which shows its aluminium skin, glowing from repeated polishings by the dedicated crew of volunteer workers. When obtained by the Arizona Wing of the CAF, the B-17G was without turrets but diligent work by the CAF has seen all three turrets restored to the airframe. Turrets, once common in most surplus scrap yards, have now become sought after collector's items—with prices ranging as high as $10,000

Classics in formation. *Sentimental Journey*
prepares for a low pass at the 1982 Madera
Gathering of Warbirds with TB-25N N7946C
(s/n 44-28938, c/n 33263)

Overleaf Gear down and in a steep bank
while turning final for landing, *Sentimental
Journey* makes an imposing sight in this May
1985 photograph. Based at Falcon Field,
Mesa, Arizona, *Sentimental Journey* regularly
visits airshows across America. A modest fee
is charged for tours of the interior of the
famous bomber and this money goes a long
way towards keeping the immaculate veteran
flying. *Journey's* nose art depicts America's
most famous WW2 pin-up, Betty Grable

Top left B-17G N3701G (s/n 44-8543) was operated for many years by Dothan Aviation in Alabama as a fire ant sprayer. These deadly ants infest the south and southwestern United States and regular dosings of poison from Dothan's two Flying Fortresses helped decrease the threat to the public. As the two Forts became more uneconomical to operate, Dothan decided to sell both planes. 'Doc' Hospers purchased N3701G and, after much work, ferried the plane back to Ft Worth, Texas. Named *Chuckie* after his wife, Hosper and Chuckie have kept the Fort in flying condition while adding military bits and pieces to make the Fort more authentic. Photographed at Breckenridge, Texas, during May 1984, this view shows interesting details such as bomb bay and covering patch over where the belly turret was installed

Far left Here's *Chuckie* three years later (May 1987), skirting around rain storms surrounding Breckenridge. During the intervening three years, *Chuckie's* crew has accomplished much—installing a top turret, polishing the airframe, adding a new nose Perspex, and installing much original military equipment in the interior

Above David Tallichet flying his B-17G during August 1985. Tallichet is the only current B-17 owner that actually flew Forts during combat, operating out of Thorpe Abbots with the 100th Bomb Group of the 8th Air Force. N3703G had been operated by TBM, Inc, as a fire bomber before being obtained by Tallichet's Yesterday's Air Force. The Flying Fortress has been painted up as an F model and is minus the G's characteristic chin turret. N3703G is s/n 44-83546, c/n 32187

Top left With bits of grass and associated airshow debris being kicked up by the props on its outboard Wright R-1820 radials (1200 hp each), the Experimental Aircraft Association's N5017N swings around into its parking spot following an early morning sortie

Left Climbing out from Titusville, Florida, in a nose-up attitude, N5017N displays the Fortress's fine lines. Donated to the EAA by a group of warbird pilots that had purchased the ageing veteran from Dothan Aviation (where it served with N3701G as a firebomber), the four-engine heavy (the prototype of which had made its first flight on 28 July 1935) is maintained in fine flying condition by the EAA

Above The graceful lines of B-17G N5017N (s/n 44-85740) will eventually be enhanced by the addition of turrets and other military equipment as the EAA finds time and funds to equip their four-engine bomber with original WW2 equipment. Most civil Forts were previously operated as fire bombers until a Forest Service directive stated that the planes were too old for such hazardous operations. This released the bombers for sale to warbird enthusiasts but, unfortunately, many perfectly fine and flyable civilian B-17s went to the USAF where they now rot outside as gate guardians at various USAF bases that are part of the USAF Museum's heritage programme. Operators received 'newer' equipment (C-118s, C-123s, etc) for conversion to fire bombers via these trades

Right The damaged Fort (as well as the destroyed example) was purchased by Aviation Specialties, Mesa, Arizona, and put in flying shape for a ferry flight back to Falcon Field. Dubbed *Yucca Lady* the Fort was rebuilt over a period of ten years by Gene Packard and his crew. 'We rebuilt the aircraft exactly to fit our operations,' recalled Packard. 'All the military equipment was junked.' Once finally finished, the bomber was used on forest fires and for spraying. Sold off in the 1986 auction, the Fort went to Bob Collings who immediately had the plane flown to Tom Reilly's 'Bombertown' near Orlando, Florida. Reilly and his large crew went to work to bring N93012 back to military condition and the result can be seen in this photograph. A top turret was still being completed and had not been installed by the time our March 1987 photograph was taken

Left One of the most recent Fortress restorations is Bob Collings' magnificent Boeing B-17G N93012 painted up as *Nine-O-Nine*, a WW2 8th Air Force Fort based in Britain. This particular airframe has a very interesting history. Last operated in USAF service by the Military Air Transport Service, the Fort, upon retirement, was flown to Nevada and used on one of the sites where atomic weapons were still (unwisely) being exploded above ground. When the weapon was detonated, another Fort nearer the explosion was torn apart but N93012 survived with blast shock wrinkles and some radiation contamination

The fabulous *Sally B*, Britain's only operational Flying Fortress, is seen on an outing from its Duxford base, operated as an extension of the Imperial War Museum and located near the university town of Cambridge. Accompanied by two warbird fighters from Stephen Grey's ever growing fleet (Stephen is flying his P-51D while Steve Hinton is at the controls of the Thunderbolt), *Sally B* is being flown by Keith Sissons. B-17G-105-VE was obtained from USAAF stocks by *Institut Geographique National*, Creil, France, where, along with twelve other Forts, the vintage B-17 was put to use in a mapping capacity. Registered F-BGSR, the Fort was obtained by the late Ted White on 20 January 1975, registered N117TE and operated on the airshow circuit. Later registered G-BEDF, the B-17G is now maintained by a preservation trust and is enthusiastically flown as the last British example of a type of aircraft that once literally darkened the skies over the island nation

The mighty Liberator, built in even greater quantities than the Flying Fortress, was the most mass-produced bombing aircraft in history . . . yet, while more widely used than the B-17, it received less than its fair share of publicity or fame. Today, the B-24 is one of our rarest warbirds . . . only a handful survive in the museum's of the world. The only true bombing version of the Liberator still flying is the B-24J owned by Yesterday's Air Force

Overleaf, inset right David Tallichet, President of Yesterday's Air Force, was well aware of the fact that the Indian Air Force had, amazingly, been operating Liberators on ocean patrol duties until the late 1960s. The Indians, instead of scrapping all the aircraft (which were replaced in their duties by almost as equally aged Constellations), made some of the airframes available to museums. Pima County Museum in Arizona received an example as well as the RAF Museum and Canadian War Museum but none of these aircraft were destined to fly again. Tallichet had other plans and had his B-24J, registered N94459, prepared for an epic flight back to America. This view shows the waist gun position with its enclosure attached. Note the wind deflector to help the gunner turn his .50 calibre weapon more easily in the slipstream

Overleaf, inset left In an epic flight, Liberator N94459 (s/n 44-44272) was flown to Duxford, England, and given lavish care by the Duxford Aviation Society. From there the bomber headed towards America (a collapsed nose gear delayed the journey) and eventually arrived at Tallichet's main base in Chino. While at Duxford, the plane had been highly polished (the Indians had left their Liberators in remarkably good and original condition—all the turrets were still in place). The B-24J's massive twin tails and rear turret are seen in this view at Chino during September 1979

Overleaf B-24J N94459 in all its glory at Chino. Unfortunately, the fortunes of the highly-polished veteran were to go down hill after arriving in the States. The Liberator attended several airshows and then slowly lapsed into a non-flying condition although several attempts have been made to get the four-engine bomber back into the air. The most recent trip saw the bomber travel from March AFB to Liberal, Kansas, where it was forced down due to engine problems. The plane is currently being repaired and made airworthy

Top left Of all the aircraft preserved by the Confederate Air Force, perhaps the most impressive is the magnificent Boeing B-29A Superfortress N4249 (s/n 44-62070, c/n 11547) which is kept in fine flying condition. Rescued from dozens of Superfortresses at China Lake Naval Air Station where they were being used as targets for weapon testing, N4249 has been kept in operational trim since being obtained by the CAF. As well as attending many airshows, the veteran bomber—America's most advanced WW2 strategic weapon—has appeared in movies and television programmes, taking a lead role in the film *The Right Stuff*

Left This is where the Confederate Air Force's Superfortress came from . . . the vast collection of B-29s assembled in the Mojave desert for target practice. This forest of aircraft shows off a wide variety of markings . . . encompassing everything from WW2 to Korea. Fortunately, the dry desert weather kept the marginally undamaged bombers in good shape (many of the 200 plus Superfortresses flown to China Lake were blasted to bits) and eventually allowed two other Superfortress to fly out. After an initial go by several museums in the 1970s, many of the Superfortresses were scrapped and, today, only two rather ragged B-29s remain at China Lake for inclusion in a planned China Lake NAS Museum

Above One of the Superfortesses that made it out 'alive' from China Lake NAS is the example currently on display at the Imperial War Museum's Duxford, England, facility. After initial restoration work was carried out on site, the big bomber was flown to Tucson, Arizona, for further restoration before making the lengthy journey to Britain. Registered as G-BHDK, TB-29A-45-BN 44-61748 had seen service with the 307th Bomb Group and flew 105 missions over Korea and is painted in appropriate markings. Unfortunately, after its ferry flight the bomber was never to fly again, enduring several harsh British winters before being moved inside the new 'big hangar' in decidedly non-airworthy condition

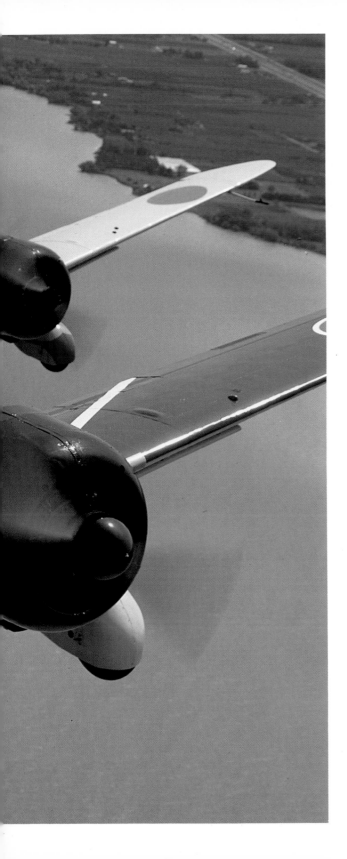

Pseudo-bombers

Costing a fortune (at the time) and receiving mostly poor reviews, the epic film *Tora! Tora! Tora!* recreated the massive Japanese attack on Pearl Harbor which took place on 7 December 1941 and propelled the United States into WW2. Most of the poor reviews were products of the time; the Vietnam War had made negative statements about any sort of military endeavour popular, and the film suffered accordingly. Viewed today, the film is actually an accurate and painstaking account of the devasting attack. One of the benefits of the film that is still with us is the fact that the producers needed an air force and, since Japanese aircraft were unobtainable, they had to create their own air arm. WW2 trainers were heavily modified to resemble enemy Vals, Kates and Zeros. Two of the modified BT-13s (Vals) are seen in formation over Hamilton, Canada

A *Tora!* Val is seen flying over Breckenridge, Texas, during May 1984. Most of the modifications to a fleet of BT-13s and Texans was undertaken by Stewart-Davis Co at Long Beach, California. Their base took on the look of a WW2 factory with the trainers receiving modifications while derelict Catalinas were cosmetically fixed to look like 1941 examples. A P-40E and Douglas Dauntless were also on the ramp for restoration but neither made it into the film although the P-40E was used to make the very realistic fibreglass Kittyhawks that were destroyed during the attack on the Army's air bases in Hawaii. Most of the surviving *Tora!* aircraft have been acquired by the Confederate Air Force for their impressive *Tora!* routine but several remain in the hands of private owners. The various modifications to create a look-alike Val are clearly seen on Vultee BT-13 Valiant N56478

Marauding Vals N56336 and N56478 are seen in formation. Fibreglass and sheet aluminium were used to create most of the modifications to the *Tora!* aircraft. Some of the Vals were equipped with swinging bomb arms that actually worked. Two of the aircraft were lost during filming in accidents while several more have been destroyed during operations in the United States

Left The replica that required the most work to create was the Kate torpedo bomber. Basically a Texan/Harvard airframe was cut into two and a new bay added to make for a longer fuselage. Completing this was the rear fuselage and tail section from a Vultee BT-13 Valiant. The front of the Texan was also extensively reworked to make the plane look more like the real Kate. Extended wing tips, a tail hook, and new canopy completed the most effective modification. John Bell II is seen flying N6438D which, at the time, was owned by Challenge Publications. A rare North American Yale is seen breaking away from the formation (now on display in the USAF Museum) while a *Tora!* Zero follows close behind

Top left Frontal view of the Val shows the convincing dive bomber replica created by Stewart-Davis. When MGM was finished with their film warriors, the aircraft were returned to Los Angeles and auctioned off—average prices being between $2000 and $4000. These were excellent bargins considering the fact that a *Tora!* Zero replica was recently advertised for sale at $50,000!

Above The Confederate Air Force's *Tora!* act is seen forming up prior to its 'attack' on Pearl Harbor (the location also masquarading as Breckenridge, Texas). Over the years, the *Tora!* performance has become just about the CAF's most popular airshow act. This view shows four of the modified Texan Zeros, a Kate, and a stock Texan painted up in Japanese markings

Over the years, some of the *Tora!* aircraft have undergone restorations and various improvements. N7062C, a freshly painted example, displays its open rear cockpit complete with machine gun. The large torpedoes were made for the movie and although they degrade performance, the torpedoes look great for airshows

Overleaf Streaming smoke from its generators, Martin Caidin's Junkers Ju-52/3m cruises leisurely over the Florida coastline. The colourful paint scheme, the smoke generators, and the underwing speakers that boomed out Nazi marching songs and ranting Hitler speeches, all combined into a really great airshow machine. Caidin, best known as a writer of aviation and science fiction thrillers, obtained the Ju-52 from a pilot who had flown the old beast out of South America where it had been operating since before WW2. Over the period of several years, Caidin lavished a small fortune on *Iron Annie*, bringing the plane back to pristine condition

N52JU in formation with a Nord-built Me-208 during the March 1983 Valiant Air Command show. During the mid-1930s, a bombing variant of the trimotor Junkers was built. Designated Ju-52/3mg3e, the plane was to be a heavy bomber with the still secret *Luftwaffe*. Carrying a crew of four and defended by two MG 15 machine guns and a load of bombs, the type saw action during the Spanish Civil War but its bombing career was fairly short—the lumbering trimotor being replaced by more modern Do-17 and He-111 aircraft as they became available. N52JU has since been sold to *Lufthansa* and of special significance to the airline since the aircraft is one of the very few surviving Junkers Ju-52/3ms. Volunteers at the airline have completely restored the trimotor back to its mid-1930s airline configuration and colours and intend to keep the old bird operational for years to come

Avenger

There's little doubt that the Grumman TBF
Avenger was one of the hardest working combat
aircraft of WW2. There's also little doubt that
surplus Avengers were some of the hardest
working ex-military aircraft—performing a wide
variety of workaday tasks including fire bombing
and bug and crop spraying. In California
particularly, Avengers were hard-worked fighting
the deadly forest and brush fires which attempt to
consume the State every summer. However, a ban
was finally instigated in the late 1960s on
operating single-engine aircraft for Forest Service
work. Most of the Avenger fleet was sold to
Canada (average price was around $5000) where
they went on to battle spruce bud worm
infestation which causes extreme damage to that
nation's valuable lumber resources. Painted Glossy
Sea Blue, Avenger NL7001C was restored by
Ralph Ponte, Grass Valley, California, for warbird
collector Gordon Plaskett

Left The Avenger is interesting in the fact that it appears portly yet rather sleek at the same time. This contradiction is probably due to the fat fuselage which housed three crewmembers, a gun turret, and the torpedo. The wing of the Avenger is large but has a rather elegant sweepback to the outer panels which helps dispel the heavy lines of the fuselage

Inset Looking like it would never fly again, TBM-3E N7835C is seen at Chino, California, on 24 November 1973. Owned by Ed Maloney's Planes of Fame Air Museum, the Avenger had been heavily vandalized while it was stored at nearby Ontario Airport. Once Maloney was able to establish a permanent base for his large collection, N6835C was brought out of storage,

repaired and restored and, today, is a regular part of the Museum's flying collection. Minus the right wing, this view shows the turret and crew entry door to advantage

Above Gordon Plaskett piloting NL7001C over King City, California. Powered by a 1700 hp Wright R-2600 radial, the Avenger has a top speed of 271 mph at 12,000 ft. All of the flying warbird Avengers today are Eastern-built TBM-3s. Eastern was the aircraft division of General Motors and took over production of the Avenger while Grumman concentrated on the Hellcat and other fighter development. Avengers stayed in Fleet service until 1954 (and longer in the Reserves)

TBM-3 N66475 was rather typical of the hard-
working Avengers used during the 1960s, before
the type acquired warbird status and, hence,
increased value. This plane has been extensively
modified as a sprayer: note the large tank placed
in the bomb bay and the spray booms under the
wings. The canopy has been cut down to a single-
place configuration. The scruffy condition is
indicative of the plane's hard-working role.
N66475 is not carried on today's civil register
which means the plane was either crashed,
scrapped, or sold in Canada

High over Breckenridge, Texas, Howard Pardue is seen airborne in TBM-3E NX88HP named *Turkeycat*. Restored to 1943 combat configuration, Howard reports that this particular aircraft was used by the military at one stage in its career for testing ejection seats. This view shows the long bomb bay to advantage, its length needed to accommodate the single torpedo for which the aircraft was designed to carry. Avengers made their debut in the Battle of Midway—six planes from VT-8 attacking the Japanese fleet, only one returning. It was not a good debut but the Avenger would go on to prove its worth as the premier US Navy torpedo bomber of WW2

Top left Probably the finest example of a restored Avenger currently flying is Dr John Kelly's TBM-3E which has been fully outfitted back to its late WW2 configuration. N9586Z has been fitted with the Avenger's normal armament of one forward firing .30 calibre machine gun, one .50 calibre in the turret, and one .30 calibre in the ventral position. Up to 1600 lbs of weapons could be carried in the bomb bay.

Left The hinged bomb bay on N9586Z is seen in the opened position. Grumman built 2290 Avengers while Eastern added another 2882 TBM-1s and 4664 TBM-3s to Navy ranks

Above The attractive planform of the Avenger's wing is seen to advantage in this high angle view to Dr Kelly's N9586Z. After the war, Avengers were modified by the Navy and used for a wide variety of tasks including airborne early warning (equipped with a huge radome under the fuselage) and as a COD transport (carrier onboard delivery, seven seat interior)

Close-up view of N9586Z illustrates the amount of detail work that brought Dr Kelly's Avenger back to such fine condition. When Avenger restorations started in the 1970s, most fire bomber bases still had some original parts left in their junk yards—items like turrets and bomb bay doors that, while having no use to the fire bombing role, were absolutely essential to restorers. These items have now become extremely difficult to find and in a recent auction a pair of very well-used bomb bay doors went for a stunning $11,000

Top left Painted in attractive Fleet Air Arm D-Day invasion markings, Bob Pond's Avenger is seen with its gear down during a May 1983 photo sortie. TBM-3E NL7075C, Buno 53785, was operated in a sprayer role by Charles Reeder, Twin Falls, Idaho, before being sold for restoration

Left Although blanked off, this view shows where the ventral .30 calibre weapon was installed immediately forward of the tail wheel. The Avenger is just one of Pond's fleet of impressively restored WW2 aircraft. Britain obtained 921 Avengers through Lend-Lease and some of the Avengers were operated well into the 1950s

Above Painted in a very dark blue camouflage, TBM-3E C-CCWG is owned and operated by the Canadian Warplane Heritage and is seen during a moment of rest at the museum's Hamilton base. Obtained from Ed Maloney during the 1970s, the Avenger was a significant addition to the museum since the TBM played a major role with the Royal Canadian Navy—some of today's surviving Avengers are ex-RCN machines that were sold surplus in the States

Skyraider

The purposeful lines of AD-4NA N409Z are seen passing over the airfield at Madera, California, during August 1986 with Jay Cullum at the controls. Created in 1944 as a contestant in the Navy's new single-east BT category of attack aircraft, the Skyraider came about during an overnight brain-storming session as Ed Heinemann, Leo Devlin and Gene Root produced sketches in their hotel room. This all-night session proved its worth as Douglas would go on to build 3180 Skyraiders over a twelve year period

There's little doubt that, during its military service, some of the most colourful markings ever carried by the Douglas Skyraider were those of the United States Navy's VA-176. 'The Stingers' insignia comprised a very angry insect thrusting its stinger along the vertical fin—an appropriate marking for the Navy's heavy-hitting Skyraider. Jay Cullum's AD-4NA N409Z is seen on the ramp at the 1986 edition of the Reno National Air Race where the big attack bomber provided a thrilling, if not exactly competitive, sight going around the pylons

The majority of surviving flyable Skyraiders in the United States are AD-4NAs, imported from France in the 1970s by warbird collector Jack Spanich. When trouble in Algeria picked up, the French found that they did not have a really efficient aircraft with which to bomb their colonists. With the immediate aid of the US government, 93 Skyraiders were quickly transferred from Navy stocks to the *Armee de l'Air*. The group comprised 40 AD-4NAs and 53 AD-4Ns (which were brought up to AD-4NA standards upon arrival in France). Serving effectively against the *Front de Liberation Nationale*, the Skyradiers were then sent to such far-flung areas as French Somaliland and the Malagassy Republic following the granting of independence to Algeria. George Baker is seen flying Harry Doan's 'battle' damaged AD-4NA NX91945 over Florida during March 1987. This aircraft was damaged in a landing accident when owned by Jack Spanich and has only recently been returned to flying status. Note the missing landing gear fairings and replacement left wing

Overleaf Heavy-hitters in formation. The March 1987 edition of the popular Valiant Air Command warbird show in Florida hosted these two ex-*Armee de l'Air* AD-4NA Skyraiders. George Baker leads the formation in NX91945 (second use of registration) while Dr Bill Harrison flies wing in NX91935. France after getting their use out of the Skyraider fleet, handed AD-4NA's over to Chad, Cambodia, and the Central African Republic but some Skyraiders remained in active service well into the 1970s

Spanning 50 feet and $\frac{1}{4}$ inch, the Skyraider was no small aircraft. Capable of carrying a huge variety of underwing weapons, the Skyraider was also armed with four 20 mm cannon in the wing. Powered by the oil-loving Wright R-3350, the AD-4NA is capable of a top speed of 320 mph (although Jay Cullum reports that his Skyraider slows down by about 45 mph when he attaches a full load of dummy rockets and bombs for airshow appearances). This view gives a good idea of the size of the Skyraider's huge four blade Aeroproducts propeller as George Baker brings NX91945 into formation with the camera plane. It is interesting note that of the small number of surviving flyable Skyraiders, three are painted in the markings of VA-176. On 21 May 1953, an AD-4B set a world weight lift record when it took off with 14,941 lbs of weapons and fuel including six 500 lb bombs, three 1000 lb bombs and six 750 lb bombs

Douglas AD-4NA NX91945 (Buno 126882) was beautifully restored in Vietnam-era markings by Jack Spanich, one of four AD-4NAs that he returned to the States from France. Photographed over Hamilton, Canada, during the annual Canadian Warplane Heritage show in June 1984, Spanich had equipped the Skyraider with underwing rockets, low drag bombs and a huge centreline fuel tank. The AD-4NA was a modification of the -4N which saw all the night attack equipment removed in order for heavier bomb loads to be carried for Korean operations. Unfortunately, Spanich and his wife died in NX91945 when the plane slammed into a mountain on 4 November 1984 near Culpepper, Virginia, while Spanich was trying to fly low to avoid bad weather

The massive lines of the Skyraider are well-portrayed in this close-up view of Pete Thelen's EA-1E, photographed during March 1984. Stated by some to be the last Skyraider in operational service with the US Navy, the EA-1E went through a couple of civilian owners, rarely flying, before being purchased by Pete. N62446 (Buno 135178) started out life as an AD-5W early warning aircraft with a huge under fuselage radar dome, an almost 2 ft fuselage stretch, and a 50 per cent larger vertical tail. Flown for the first time on 17 August 1951, the AD-5 was developed into a number of different variants including the AD-5N night attack ariant, AD-5Q ECM platform, and AD-5W early warning variant. Douglas built 218 AD-5Ws

The EA-1E looks a bit awkward with its gear coming down—somewhat in the style of the Curtiss P-40 retraction system. The EA-1E has a large 'hump back' that originally accommodated four seats (including pilot) for the craft's EW role. During the 1962 Tri-Service designation consolidation, the AD-5W became the EA-1E

Overleaf During the 1960s, most surviving EA-1Es were heavily modified with the removal of the ugly radome and modification of the crew housing, usually having blue-tinted throw-over hatches added for better visibility. The USAF produced 150 A-1Es and had them extensively modified for the Air Commando role in Southeast Asia. The Royal Navy also received 50 AD-4Ws beginning in November 1951. Today, N62446 is owned and operated by the Lone Star Aviation Museum in Houston, Texas